EASY WAY TO GU

B

THE MAJOR SCALE

A SCALE IS A SERIES OF TONES IN ALPHABETICAL ORDER. ALL MAJOR SCALES HAVE EIGHT TONES AND ARE CONSTRUCTED IN THE SAME PATTERN:

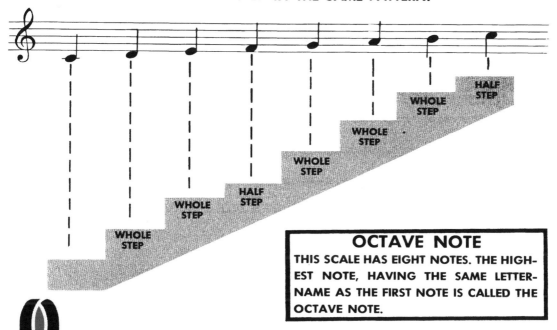

> ### OCTAVE NOTE
> THIS SCALE HAS EIGHT NOTES. THE HIGHEST NOTE, HAVING THE SAME LETTER-NAME AS THE FIRST NOTE IS CALLED THE OCTAVE NOTE.

www.melbay.com/93195BCDEB

Online Audio

THE KEY OF C

ALL MUSIC STUDIED SO FAR IN THIS BOOK HAS BEEN IN THE KEY OF C. THAT MEANS THAT THE NOTES HAVE BEEN TAKEN FROM THE C SCALE (SHOWN BELOW) AND MADE INTO MELODIES.

IT IS CALLED THE C SCALE BECAUSE THE FIRST NOTE IS C AND WE PROCEED THROUGH THE MUSICAL ALPHABET UNTIL C REAPPEARS. C - D - E - F - G - A - B - C.

WE WILL COVER THE SUBJECT OF KEYS AND SCALES MORE THOROUGHLY IN THE THEORY AND HARMONY CHAPTERS APPEARING LATER ON IN THIS COURSE. AT PRESENT WE WILL DEAL ONLY WITH BASIC FUNDAMENTALS.

THE C SCALE

WHEN A SCALE IS WRITTEN WITH THE ½ STEPS FROM THE 3RD TO 4TH AND 7TH TO 8TH STEPS OF THE SCALE, IT IS A MAJOR SCALE, AND IS GIVEN THE NAME OF THE FIRST NOTE.

3 4 5 6 7 8 9 0

MW00562135

FOUR-NOTE CHORDS

WE USE THE SAME METHOD FOR BUILDING FOUR-NOTE CHORDS AS WE DID IN BUILDING THE THREE NOTE CHORDS. PLAY THE FOUR NOTES HOLDING THE FINGERS DOWN UNTIL CHORD IS REACHED. STRIKE THEM TOGETHER PRODUCING THE CHORD.

A FOUR-NOTE CHORD STUDY

GOOD BYE OLD PAINT

Track #2

(3RD FINGER)

2

A REVIEW OF SHARPS, FLATS, AND NATURALS

LET US REVIEW THE FOLLOWING RULES:

1. A SHARP (♯) BEFORE A NOTE RAISES THE PITCH ONE FRET.

2. A FLAT (♭) BEFORE A NOTE LOWERS THE PITCH ONE FRET.

3. A NATURAL (♮) BEFORE A NOTE RESTORES IT TO ITS ORIGINAL POSITION.

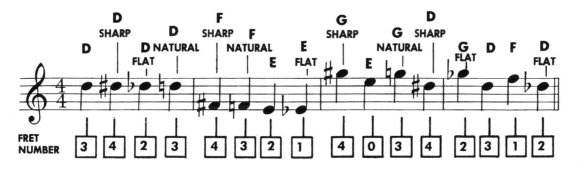

COMPLETE THE FOLLOWING NOTE STUDY

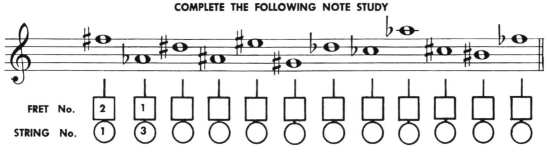

AN IMPORTANT RULE

A SHARP, FLAT, OR NATURAL SIGN PLACED BEFORE A NOTE REMAINS IN EFFECT FOR THE DURATION OF THE MEASURE UNLESS NOTES THAT FOLLOW ARE MARKED OTHERWISE BY USE OF ACCIDENTALS.

1. NOTES THAT HAVE BEEN CIRCLED ARE STILL AFFECTED BY THE SHARP SIGNS.

2. NOTES THAT HAVE BEEN CIRCLED ARE STILL AFFECTED BY THE FLAT SIGNS.

3. NOTES THAT ARE CIRCLED HAVE BEEN RESTORED TO THEIR ORIGINAL POSITION BY NATURALS.

THE "C" CHORD

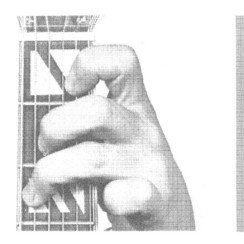

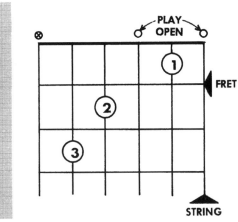

PLAY OPEN

FRET

STRING

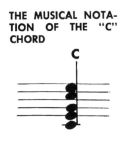

THE MUSICAL NOTATION OF THE "C" CHORD

⊗ = INDICATES THAT THE STRING IS TO BE OMITTED.

C CHORD STUDY

// = REPEAT THE SAME CHORD

"C" CHORD STUDY WITH THE ALTERNATE BASS

HOLD THE FIRST AND SECOND FINGERS DOWN THROUGH THE ENTIRE STUDY. THE THIRD FINGER ALTERNATES FROM THE C-NOTE TO THE G-NOTE. (5TH AND 6TH STRINGS).

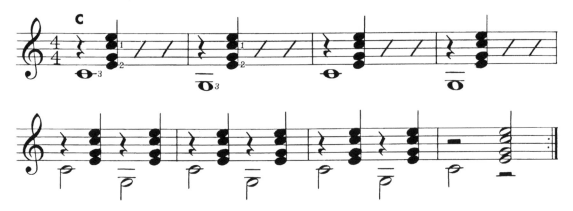

A "C" CHORD STUDY IN ¾ TIME USING THE ALTERNATE BASS. HOLD FIRST AND SECOND FINGERS DOWN THROUGHOUT.

GYMNASTICS

TO BECOME A GOOD GUITARIST, THE FOLLOWING STUDIES MUST BE MASTERED.

THE DOWN STROKE (⊓) SHOULD BE USED.

LATER USE THE DOWN-UP STROKE (⊓V).

START SLOWLY GAINING SPEED THROUGH PRACTICE.

HOLD FIRST FINGER DOWN (X----) THROUGHOUT EACH STUDY.

REPEAT EACH STUDY FOUR TIMES.

ONE-TWO

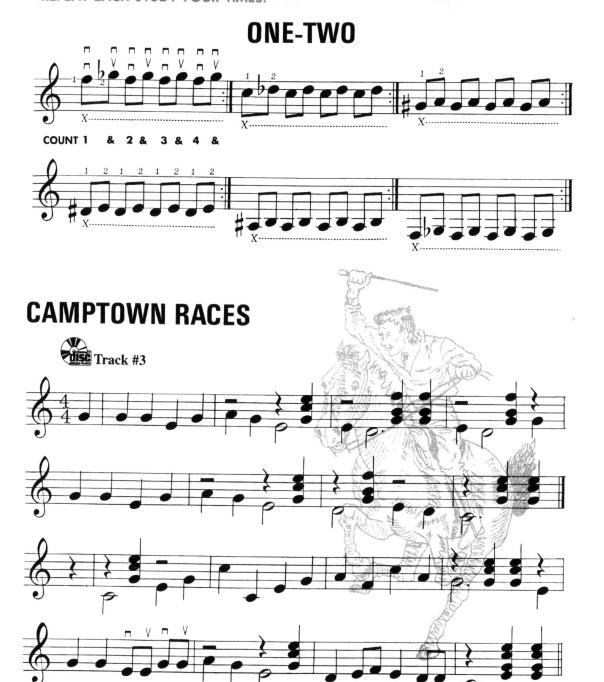

COUNT 1   &   2   &   3   &   4   &

CAMPTOWN RACES

Track #3

5

THE G7 CHORD

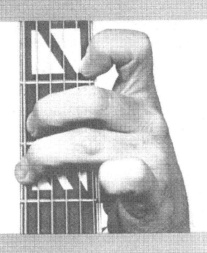

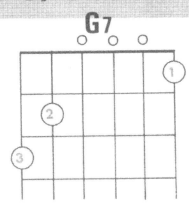

MUSICAL NOTATION

G7 TO C CHORD STUDY

THE G7 CHORD WITH THE ALTERNATE BASS NOTE (D)

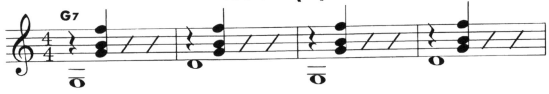

C AND G7 CHORD STUDY

LET US SING
AND PLAY
OUR FIRST SONG
(USING THE C AND G7 CHORDS)

Track #4 **LONG, LONG AGO**

◆ = BASS NOTE OF THE CHORD   / / / = STROKES OF THE PICK

Tell — me the tales — that to me — were so dear — — —

Long — long a - go — — — long — long a - go — — —

Sing — me the song — I de - light - ed to hear — — —

Long — long a - go — — — long — long a - go. — —

BE SURE TO PLAY THE BASS NOTES AND CHORDS DIRECTLY ON EACH WORD OR SYLLABLE AS INDICATED.

7

GYMNASTIC No. 2

THIS STUDY WILL DEVELOP THE FIRST AND THIRD FINGERS. BE SURE TO HOLD THE FIRST FINGER DOWN AT ALL TIMES. DO NOT RAISE YOUR FIRST FINGER UNTIL YOU CHANGE OVER TO ANOTHER STRING.

ONE-THREE

Track #5

THE ASH GROVE

8

THE "F" CHORD

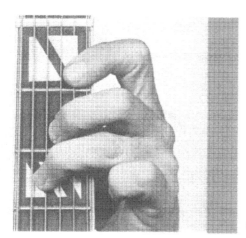

F

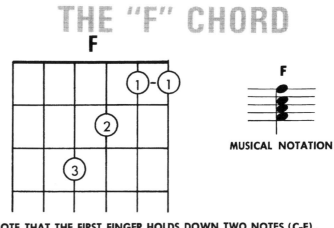

F

MUSICAL NOTATION

*NOTE THAT THE FIRST FINGER HOLDS DOWN TWO NOTES (C-F).

DEVELOPING THE "F" CHORD

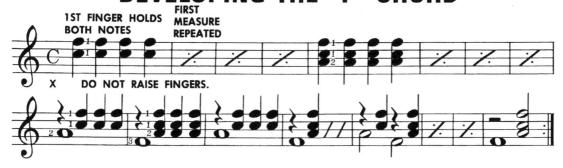

1ST FINGER HOLDS BOTH NOTES — FIRST MEASURE REPEATED

DO NOT RAISE FINGERS.

SMALL CHORD ETUDE

ACCOMPANIMENT STYLES

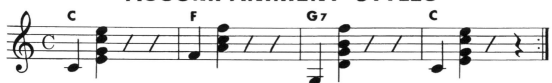

ALTERNATE BASSES

IN THREE-FOUR TIME

THE C, F AND G7 CHORDS ARE THE PRINCIPAL CHORDS IN THE KEY OF C.

MASTER THE FOLLOWING CHORD STUDY:
REPEAT UNTIL NO TIME IS LOST IN CHANGING.

REMEMBER THAT YOU SHOULD NEVER
RAISE A FINGER UNTIL IT IS NECESSARY.

SING AND PLAY

GYMNASTIC No. 3

THE GENTLE MAIDEN

Track #7

ENGLISH FOLK SONG

(HOLD FINGERS)

RITARD

RITARD = SLOW DOWN.

= GLIDE PICK SLOWLY OVER THE STRINGS.

= PAUSE OR HOLD — GIVING MORE TIME TO THE NOTES UNDERNEATH.

11

T O N E

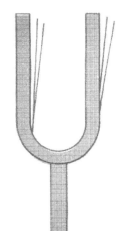

MUSIC IS COMPOSED OF SOUNDS PLEASANT TO THE EAR.

SOUND MAY BE MADE FROM NOISE OR TONE.

NOISE IS MADE BY IRREGULAR VIBRATIONS SUCH AS WOULD BE CAUSED BY STRIKING A TABLE WITH A HAMMER, THE SHOT OF A GUN, OR SLAPPING TWO STONES TOGETHER.

TONE IS PRODUCED BY REGULAR VIBRATIONS AS WOULD BE CAUSED BY DRAWING A BOW OVER THE STRINGS OF A VIOLIN, STRIKING THE STRINGS OF A GUITAR, OR BLOWING THROUGH A WIND INSTRUMENT, SUCH AS A TRUMPET.

A TONE HAS FOUR CHARACTERISTICS

PITCH: THE HIGHNESS OR LOWNESS OF A TONE.

DURATION: THE LENGTH OF A TONE.

DYNAMICS: THE FORCE OR POWER OF A TONE. (loudness or softness).

TIMBRE: QUALITY OF THE TONE.

A NOTE REPRESENTS THE PITCH AND DURATION OF A TONE.

Track #8   **THE WALTZING GUITAR**

GUITAR SOLO   BY MEL BAY

SING AND PLAY
THE MARINES SONG

Track #9

Solo

From the halls— of — Mon - te — zu — —

ma - To the shores of — Trip - o — li — — — We will

fight— our — Coun - try's— bat — — tles— in the air— on —

land — and — sea — — — — — First to fight— for —

right— and — free — — — dom— and to keep— our — hon - or —

clean — — — — We are proud— to — claim— the — ti — —

tle — of U — nit — ed — States— Ma rines— — — — —

TEMPO

TEMPO IS THE RATE OF SPEED OF A MUSICAL COMPOSITION.
THREE TYPES OF TEMPO USED IN THIS BOOK WILL BE:

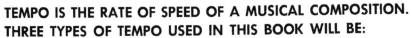

ANDANTE: A SLOW EASY PACE.

MODERATO: MODERATE.

ALLEGRO: LIVELY.

PLAYTIME

Track #10

GUITAR DUET

PLEYEL

MODERATO

ARR. BY MEL BAY

GYMNASTIC No. 4
TWO-THREE
HOLD SECOND FINGER DOWN THROUGHOUT.

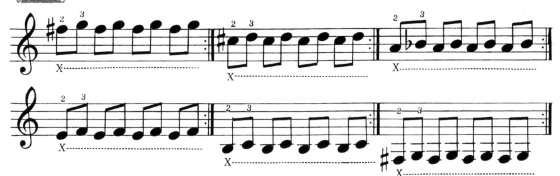

 Track #11

A WALK IN THE WOODS

MODERATO

COUNT: 1 2 & 3 4   1 2 & 3 4

GYMNASTIC NO. 5
TWO-FOUR

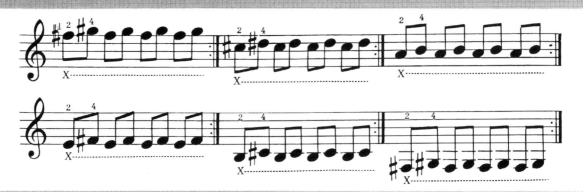

DRINK TO ME ONLY
WITH THINE EYES

Track #12

16

GYMNASTIC No. 6
THREE-FOUR

HOLD THE THIRD FINGER DOWN THROUGHOUT.

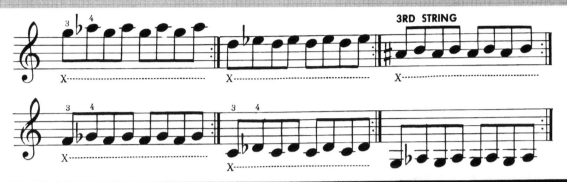

"TRACK MEET"

MEL BAY

COUNT: 1 & 2 & 3 & 4 &

THE ABOVE STUDY SHOULD BE PLAYED SLOWLY WITH A GRADUAL INCREASE OF SPEED UNTIL A MODERATE TEMPO HAS BEEN REACHED. IT IS AN EXCELLENT DAILY EXERCISE.

Track #13 # THE BLUE BELLS OF SCOTLAND

GUITAR SOLO

ARR. BY MEL BAY

THE KEY OF A MINOR

(RELATIVE TO C MAJOR)

EACH MAJOR KEY WILL HAVE A RELATIVE MINOR KEY. THE RELATIVE MINOR SCALE IS BUILT UPON THE SIXTH TONE OF THE MAJOR SCALE. THE KEY SIGNATURE OF BOTH WILL BE THE SAME.

THE MINOR SCALE WILL HAVE THE SAME NUMBER OF TONES (7) AS THE MAJOR.

THE DIFFERENCE BETWEEN THE TWO SCALES IS THE ARRANGEMENT OF THE WHOLE-STEPS AND HALF-STEPS.

THERE ARE THREE FORMS OF THE MINOR SCALE: 1. PURE OR NATURAL, 2. HARMONIC, 3. MELODIC.

THE A MINOR SCALE – NATURAL (Pure)

HARMONIC

THE 7TH TONE IS RAISED ONE HALF-STEP ASCENDING AND DESCENDING.

MELODIC

THE 6TH AND 7TH TONES ARE RAISED ONE HALF-STEP ASCENDING AND LOWERED BACK TO THEIR NORMAL PITCH DESCENDING.

Track #14   ## "SAD SACK"

THE UP STROKE

V = UP STROKE

THIS STROKE WILL BE USED ON REPEATED EIGHTH-NOTES OF THE SAME PITCH.

A VISIT TO THE RELATIVES

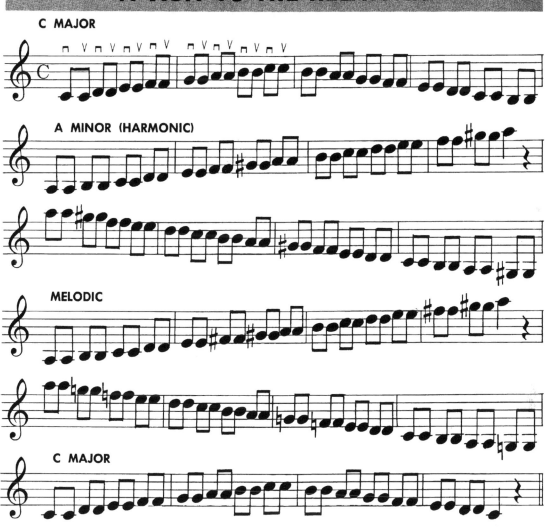

THE A MINOR CHORD
(M = MINOR)

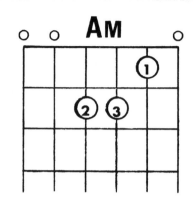

MUSICAL NOTATION

A MINOR CHORD STUDY
(PLACE FINGERS BEFORE PLAYING & HOLD THROUGHOUT STUDY)

WITH ALTERNATE BASS NOTE

IN 3/4 TIME

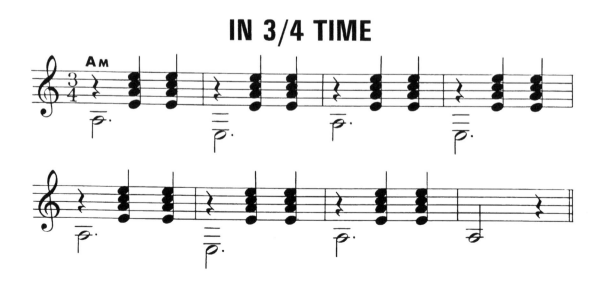

"TWO-FOUR" TIME

$\frac{2}{4}$ = TWO BEATS PER MEASURE

$\frac{2}{4}$ = QUARTER-NOTE (♩) RECEIVES ONE BEAT

TWO-FOUR TIME WILL HAVE TWO BEATS PER MEASURE WITH THE QUARTER NOTE RECEIVING ONE BEAT.

A TWO-FOUR SCALE STUDY

COUNT: 1 2   1 2   1 & 2 &

SENORITA

Track #15

GUITAR SOLO
ANDANTE

COUNT:

RITARD.

21

# THE D MINOR CHORD
DM=D MINOR CHORD

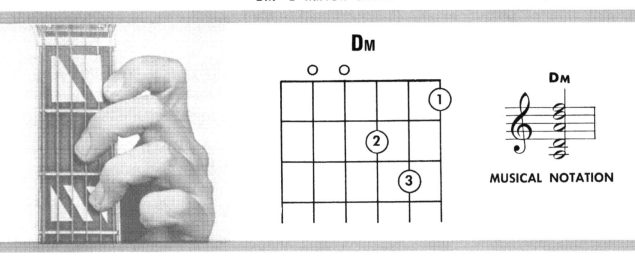

MUSICAL NOTATION

A DM CHORD STUDY

USING ALTERNATE BASS NOTE

IN THREE-FOUR TIME

IN TWO-FOUR TIME

TRIPLETS

HOW TO COUNT TRIPLETS

COUNT: 1 2 1 2 1 TRIP-LET 2 TRIP-LET 1 2

Q. WHAT THE TRIPLETS?
A. A GROUP OF THREE NOTES, PLAYED IN THE TIME OF TWO NOTES OF THE SAME KIND.

TRIPLET-EIGHTS EQUAL TO EIGHTHS

PLAY IT LIKE YOU SAY IT — 1 TRIPLET, 2 TRIPLET

TRIPLET DUET

 Track #16

*GO BACK TO THE BEGINNING AND PLAY TO THE WORD "FINE". PUPIL TO PRACTICE BOTH PARTS.

THE E7 CHORD

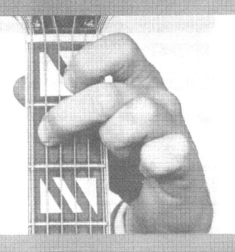

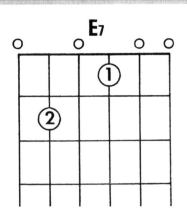

MUSICAL NOTATION

AN E7 CHORD STUDY

WITH ALTERNATE BASS NOTE

THREE-FOUR TIME

TWO-FOUR TIME

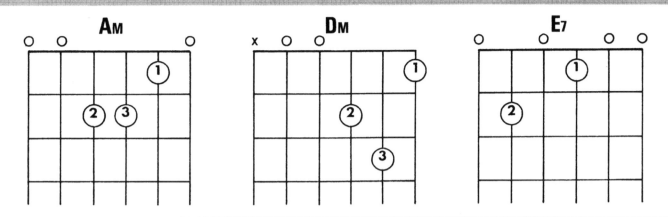

ACCOMPANIMENT STYLES IN A MINOR

ORCHESTRATION STYLE

THE DIAGONAL LINE (/) INDICATES A CHORD-STROKE. THEY WILL FALL ONLY ON EACH BEAT OF THE MEASURE.

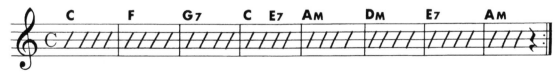

IN THE ABOVE EXERCISE NO BASS IS USED . . . ONLY THE CHORDS. REPEAT THE ACCOMPANIMENT EXERCISES UNTIL THEY CAN BE PLAYED WITHOUT MISSING A BEAT.

"DARK EYES"

Track #18

"SUNRISE"

GUITAR DUET   MEL BAY

GYMNASTIC No. 7
ONE-THREE-TWO-THREE

THE INDIAN MAIDEN

Track #19

GUITAR SOLO
MODERATO

MEL BAY

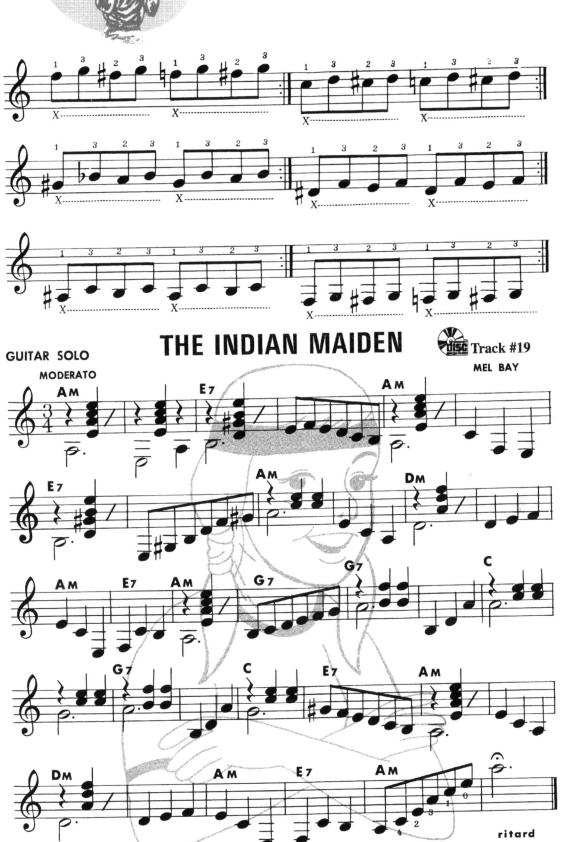

ritard

THE CHORD SYMBOLS ARE THE ACCOMPANIMENT CHORDS.

Track #20

FROLIC

GUITAR DUET

STUDENT SHOULD PLAY BOTH PARTS.

MEL BAY

ALLEGRETTO

COUNT: 1 & 2 &

28

GYMNASTIC No. 8
ONE-FOUR-THREE-FOUR

disc Track #21

TENNIS MATCH

GUITAR DUET

Fine

D.C. al Fine

29

THE KEY OF G

IT WILL BE IDENTIFIED
BY THIS SIGNATURE

THE KEY OF G WILL HAVE ONE SHARP. (F#).

THE F-NOTE WILL BE PLAYED AS SHOWN:

2ND FRET   4TH FRET   2ND FRET

2ND FINGER   4TH FINGER   2ND FINGER

THE G SCALE

NOTE THAT IN ORDER TO HAVE THE HALF-STEPS FALLING BETWEEN THE SEVENTH AND EIGHTH DEGREES OF THE SCALE THE F MUST BE SHARPED.

OUR MAJOR SCALE PATTERN IS THEN CORRECT. (1,1,½,1,1,1,½.) (STEPS)

THE GALWAY PIPER

IRISH TUNE   Track #22

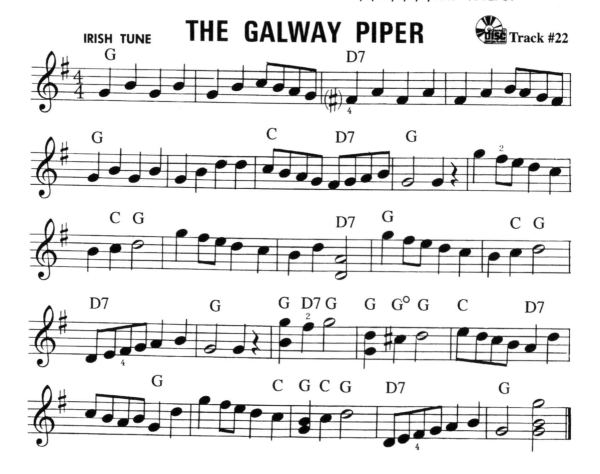

THE G CHORD

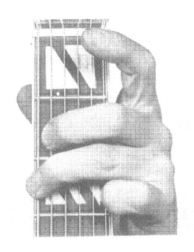

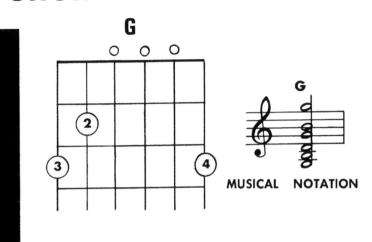

MUSICAL NOTATION

G CHORD STUDY

USING ALTERNATE BASS

IN THREE-FOUR TIME

IN TWO-FOUR TIME

THE OLD MILL

GUITAR DUET    Track #23

MODERATO

MEL BAY

I

II

FINE

I

II

I

II

D. C. AL FINE

Track #24 GERMAN FOLK SONG

THE D7 CHORD

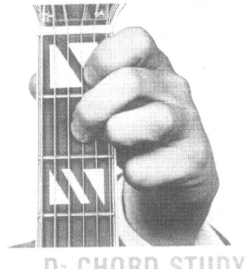

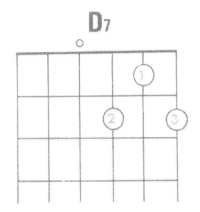

D7 CHORD STUDY

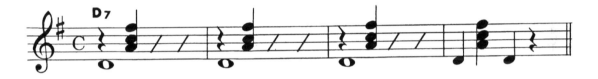

WITH ALTERNATE BASS

IN THREE-FOUR TIME

IN TWO-FOUR TIME

CHORDS IN THE KEY OF G

THE CHORDS IN THE KEY OF G ARE . . G, C, AND D7.

ACCOMPANIMENT STYLES IN THE KEY OF G

WITH ALTERNATE BASSES

IN THREE-FOUR TIME

IN TWO-FOUR TIME

WALTZ

Track #25

IRISH MELODY

34

PLAY AND SING

SHE'LL BE COMING ROUND THE MOUNTAIN

Track #26

FOR MORE FUN SEE <u>FUN WITH THE GUITAR</u> BY MEL BAY

THE FOLLOWING ETUDE INTRODUCES THE NOTES D AND B BEING PLAYED TOGETHER. THIS IS DONE BY PLAYING THE NOTE D WITH THE FIRST FINGER ON THE THIRD FRET OF THE SECOND STRING AND PLAYING THE NOTE B WITH THE SECOND FINGER UPON THE FOURTH FRET OF THE THIRD STRING.

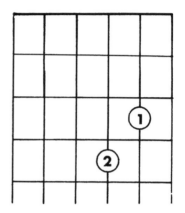

 Track #27

SLEIGH RIDE

PLAY AND SING

HAND ME DOWN

MY WALKING CANE

Track #28

IN ORDER TO START YOUR SONG IN THE CORRECT KEY, STRUM THE PRINCIPAL CHORD LIGHTLY BEFORE BEGINNING. IN THE ABOVE SONG THE PRINCIPAL OR TONIC CHORD IS G.

THE KEY OF E MINOR

(RELATIVE TO G MAJOR)
THE KEY OF E MINOR WILL HAVE THE SAME KEY SIGNATURE AS G MAJOR.

TWO E MINOR SCALES

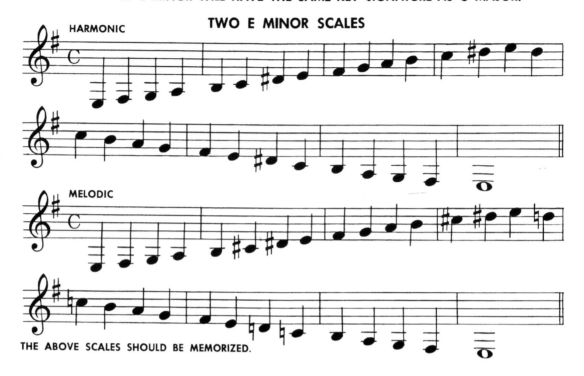

THE ABOVE SCALES SHOULD BE MEMORIZED.

Track #29 **THE LITTLE PRINCE**

GUITAR DUET

MAZAS
ARR. BY MEL BAY

ANDANTE

38

THE E MINOR CHORD

Em

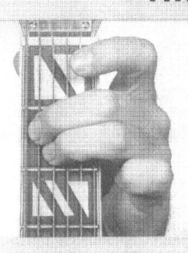

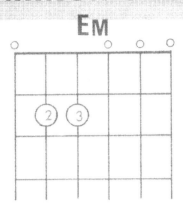

MUSICAL NOTATION

Em CHORD STUDY

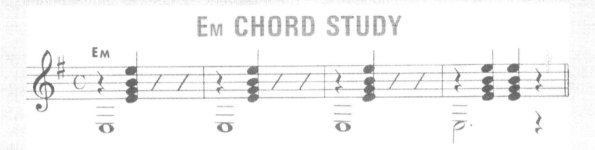

USING ALTERNATE BASS

IN THREE-FOUR TIME

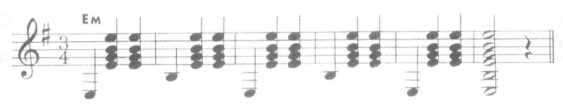

IN TWO-FOUR TIME

DOTTED QUARTER NOTES
A DOT AFTER A NOTE INCREASES ITS VALUE BY ONE-HALF.

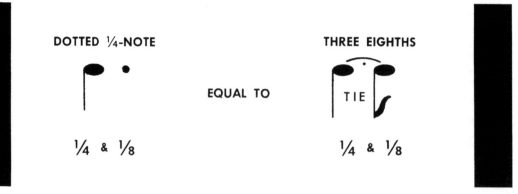

DOTTED ¼-NOTE   EQUAL TO   THREE EIGHTHS

¼ & ⅛   ¼ & ⅛

THE COUNT FOR THE DOTTED QUARTER-NOTE IS AS FOLLOWS:

A DOTTED QUARTER-NOTE ETUDE

ALL DOWN STROKE.
MELODIC

G MAJOR

SEE THE MEL BAY FOLIO OF GRADED GUITAR SOLOS
VOLUME ONE

THE B₇ CHORD

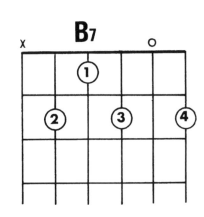

B₇

MUSICAL NOTATION

B₇ CHORD STUDY

USING ALTERNATE BASS

IN THREE-FOUR TIME

IN TWO-FOUR TIME

IN OLD SPAIN  Track #30

THE GAUCHOS Track #31

GUITAR SOLO

ALLEGRO

FINE

42

GYMNASTIC No. 9
TWO-THREE-FOUR-THREE

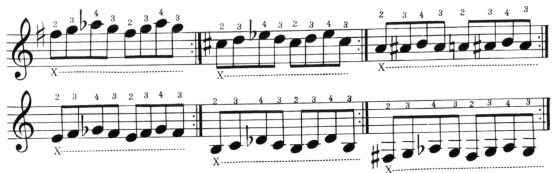

THE CHORDS IN THE KEY OF E MINOR

THE CHORDS IN THE KEY OF E MINOR ARE **EM, AM** AND **B7**.

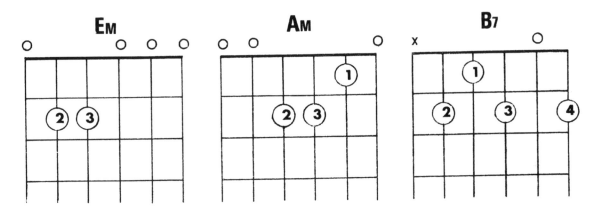

ACCOMPANIMENT STYLES IN THE KEY OF E MINOR

WITH ALTERNATE BASS

ORCHESTRATION STYLES

GYMNASTIC No. 10
ONE-THREE-TWO-FOUR

DO NOT RAISE A FINGER UNTIL THE FOUR-NOTE SET IS COMPLETED.

Track #32

"THE SAD GUITAR"

GUITAR SOLO
SLOW

MEL BAY

RITARD

GUITAR DUET

A COLONIAL DANCE

MAZAS, OP. 85

ALLEGRO

Track #33

ARR. BY MEL BAY

count: 1 & 2 &   1 2   1 & 2 &   1 2   1 & 2 &

45

AUSTRIAN HYMN

Track #34

GUITAR DUET

ANDANTE

HAYDEN
ARR. BY MEL BAY

A TRIPLE PLAY  Track #35

Track #36

MARCH OF THE GIANTS

47

Track #37 # MAYTIME

GUITAR DUET

WANHALL-BAY

Count: 1 2 3 &

Track #38 ## AN OLD MELODY

PROCEED TO BOOK "C" OF THIS COURSE

Made in the USA
San Bernardino, CA
16 October 2016